HARRY SMITH: *MAGIC MOMENTS*

HARRY SMITH: *MAGIC MOMENTS*

Introduction by Anita Ventura Mozley

Edited and with captions by Stephen White

Stephen White Editions

For Mus, Shannon and Annie.
At last . . . a book!!!

Stephen White Editions
752 North La Cienega Boulevard
Los Angeles, California 90069

First printing: September 1981

Designed by Peter A. Andersen
Composition by Instant Type, Monterey, California
Printed by Gardner/Fulmer Lithograph, Buena Park,
California
Bound by Roswell Bookbinding, Phoenix, Arizona

Manufactured in the United States of America
Library of Congress Catalogue Number 81-90385
International Standard Book Number 0-9606808-0-2
Frontispiece: *The Reluctant Child, c. 1905*

Preface

I first came to know the work of Harry Adolph Smith when I purchased a collection of his negatives in 1976. The Southern California bookshop which had owned them sold the glass plate negatives as a collection of "earthquake" pictures. In part this was true since there were some forty or fifty 4 by 5-inch glass negatives dealing with the 1906 San Francisco earthquake. They were good photographs, better than most of the other earthquake pictures I had seen. Harry Smith's other work, though — his portraits, landscapes, architectural shots and photographs of early 20th century life in California — intrigued me even more. It made me wonder who he was and why he had recorded the particular subjects he did.

I had contact prints made from the negatives, and on trips to San Francisco I began searching records at the California Historical Society and the San Francisco Hall of Records for information about the man who had taken the photographs. These investigations all led to a dead end. My Harry Smith was buried among many Harry Smiths who had lived out their lives in the city by the Golden Gate. I then remembered that the Southern California book dealer from whom I had purchased the negatives had mentioned they originally bought them at a garage sale in Marin County. My last hope was the Marin County Courthouse.

Since I did not know when, or even if, Harry Smith had died, I poured through the records of Marin County residents until I noticed the death certificates of Harry and Agnes Smith. He had died in 1973, his wife two years later. Their next of kin was listed as a son, Robert. After locating him and explaining my mission on the telephone, Robert agreed to let me visit him. He and his wife showed me an album of photographs his father had put together many years earlier. They also shared what they knew of Harry Smith's background, and of the importance photography had played in his life.

Despite my initial enthusiasm about Harry Smith's photographs, the demands of my business forced me to put the project aside. Five years later, near the end of 1980, I again looked through the Smith photographs. During those five years the general public's interest in photography had expanded at a rapid pace. Photographs were no longer viewed as mere useless objects, but as pieces of information that kept us in touch with our past in a way words could never do. Photography had become accepted as a fine art by a large segment of the population and the photographic market attracted an ever-widening group of collectors. Prints sold at auction brought record prices; major magazines such as *Time* and *Newsweek* included articles about photographers and exhibitions as standard features. Museums expanded their collections and research on photographic history increased.

During the late 1970s my own knowledge about photography had grown considerably. I had seen thousands of photographs and had learned much more about the various periods of the medium's growth and development. One evening, as I looked through the prints I had made from the negatives five years earlier, the Harry Smith pictures looked different to me. They stood out from the many albums of amateur work I had seen. Harry Smith had made these pictures for himself, for his family, without higher aspirations. His pictorial world was defined by where he lived and where he vacationed.

I felt then, and do even more strongly today as the project nears completion, that the work of Harry Smith fills a small gap in the history of photography. By the time Smith began to take pictures photography had become accessible to the middle classes, to those individuals who could use the camera to record their lives and the world around them. His vision — the way he photographed and the subjects he chose — are both foreign and familiar to us. His time is not our time, but his way of composing his photographs, his subject matter and his ability to capture the moments of his life reach out across time in a way the modern world can understand.

Photography has undergone many changes since Harry Smith's time. The painterly style dominated camera-club photography until the late 1930s, even though innovative purists such as Paul Strand, Edward Weston and Imogen Cunningham, following the lead of Alfred Stieglitz, abandoned that style for a more straightforward photographic direction. In the 1950s, first Robert Frank, then Garry Winogrand and Lee Friedlander pioneered a reemergence of the commonplace as the subject of their pictures, an approach carried on by many contemporary art photographers. The acceptance by museums, collectors and photographers of recording the everyday world gives a new role to antecedents, to Harry Smith and the other amateurs from the early years of photography who integrated composition and imagination in their pictures of ordinary situations.

Each photograph in this book had a personal significance for the photographer. Today, however, with the renewed interest in photographs of the commonplace, they may be interpreted differently from the way they were intended. Harry Smith's photographs were direct and innocent. It is these qualities that speak to us today.

Stephen White
Los Angeles, August 1981

Photography for the Love of It:
Harry A. Smith and Others

Anita Ventura Mozley

". . . Photography tends more than any other art to stimulate observation of both common and uncommon things and events."

W.F. Carlton, *The Amateur Photographer*, 1899

Harry A. Smith's only teacher in photography was W.F. Carlton, author of *The Amateur Photographer, A Complete Guide for Beginners in the Art-Science of Photography*. Carlton taught Harry Smith and thousands of American novices like him through the pages of his pamphlet, which was furnished, as the expression was then, by the Rochester Optical Company to purchasers of its Premo A camera. Smith's copy, its open pages indelibly stained with symmetrical blots, sepia Rorschach patterns formed when Harry spilled hypo under the red lamp of his darkroom, is dated 1899. By then *The Amateur Photographer* was in its twentieth edition, much revised from its initial issue seventeen years earlier. It is a charming little manual, with exhortations to taste and intelligence freely mingled with methods and formulas

tested by experience — "The commonplace is always attractive when well-treated," as well as the very practical hint that "A quill pen makes a capital lifter for the plate during development." Harry Smith took Carlton to heart and put his manual to use. Besides the stains and the rusting staples, it bears the marks he made with a firmly held black pencil. "Take time for focusing," advises Carlton, and "check" responds Smith, thus singling out for his special attention the already emphatic injunction of the Futura Bold type. Was focusing an early bugaboo of Harry Smith's? He was about seventeen when he bought his Premo A, and he wore thick glasses. He did, however, as the photographs on the following pages show, finally master that initial problem.

"Photography is almost entirely the product of amateur effort and experiment." Every beginner, Smith included, must have thrilled to these introductory words of Carlton's as he accepted the author's invitation to join that investigative and experimental crowd. Carlton's statement may seem to some a large claim, but it is in fact well-founded. For when photography was new, all photographers were amateurs. William Henry Fox

Talbot, the inventor of the positive-negative process, can be named as the first. He sought a process "by which natural objects may be made to delineate themselves without the aid of the artist's pencil." By 1835, he had achieved his unpencilled picture, a picture drawn by the sun. He thought of the picture as a piece of "natural magic"; his work as simply lifting a portion of the veil that blinds men to an understanding of the infinite ways in which nature might be made to perform her magic.

"You make the powers of nature work for you, and no wonder that your work is well and quickly done . . . you set the instrument in action, the alloted time elapses, and you find the picture finished, in every part, and in every minute particular." He assured his readers (perhaps it was surprising even to him) that complex subjects took no longer than simple ones when they were drawn by nature's laws. To him, everyday occurences were essential portions of "the same wonderful Whole" . . . "What is Nature," he asked, "but one great field of Wonders?" The wonder, the sense of magic, the delight and amazement that it should all turn out to be so, these are the emotions one experiences in any new venture; they are the emotions of the beginning amateur. The fatigue and boredom bred of repetition have not set in; there is no competition to be met, except that interposed by the process and one's own ambitions. Success seems miraculous, and every step of the way an adventure.

"I know of few things in the range of science more surprising than the gradual appearance of the picture on the blank sheet, especially the first time the experience is witnessed," Talbot wrote in the late 1830s. W. F. Carlton, writing about forty years later, stirred his students to action with a similar observation, urging them, "Now watch closely . . . As the first faint outlines appear, under the influence of the Developer, wonder grows into amazement at the change going on under one's very eyes. Outlines of familiar objects come out, as first the mast, then the hull, then the rigging and the cords of a great vessel come to us from out the dimness of a fog." This particular choice of image must have struck Harry Smith, living as he did in the greatest port of the West at a time when full-rigged ships emerged daily, cords and all, out of the fog that shrouded the Golden Gate in summer. Carlton believed that watching the miracle of development would repay all the effort, all the "labor, care and taste" the amateur would invest in producing the print.

In the early days of photography, nature, not the photographer, was always acknowledged as the maker. The photographer and the camera combined to be the medium. This must seem to be so for all amateurs of photography, who recapitulate for themselves the beginnings of the art-science. Joseph Nicéphore Niepce, having produced in 1826 what is acknowledged as the first photograph, later pondered over a possible name for the astounding phenomenon to which he had been the first witness. He drew up a list, and unlike Daguerre, who called his discovery the "Daguerreotype," he kept his own name out of it. Should it be "Painting by nature herself," "Copy by nature herself," "Portrait by nature herself?" Or, veering away a bit from nature's authorship and focusing more on the process by which she was revealed, he tried out, "To show nature herself," "Real nature," and "True copy of nature."

This self-effacement continued for a few years until art, on one hand, and commerce, on the other, set in. All photographers, even those who became professionals, started as amateurs. It is hard to believe now, but some of the most prominent of today's photographers began with box Brownies. The dividing line is crossed when the amateur is gripped by a determination to excell artistically and technically, to please others as much as he has pleased himself, or to turn his hobby into a living. These are social ambitions, and they naturally raise constraints as what has been fun becomes serious. In 1864, when Julia Margaret Cameron produced a portrait she called *Annie — My First Success,* she felt as if Annie alone had made it and ran around her house looking for gifts for the child who had provided Mrs. Cameron with what before had been so elusive. But in 1869, when George Frederick Watts remarked on her photograph *The Dream,* and she had his "Quite Divine!" made into a rubber stamp with which she marked the mounts of the prints she sold at Colnaghi's, she had become a professional artist-photographer. She was using the laws of nature to express herself.

She was exceptional among Victorian amateurs, more determined than most to make a public splash. The goal of most of these photographers was simpler; it differed little from Harry Smith's goals, although over a quarter of a century separated their efforts. What was sought was a clear and recognizable picture of something each admired, or was interested in recording. The picture should be pleasing in composition, which required a certain sensitivity to form, and rich in suggested volume, which called for technical proficiency. Although the goal was simple, the process in those early days was difficult. After the initial mastery of the laws of chemistry and optics in the late 1830s and early 1840s, came attempts at refinement — a search for more sensitive chemicals, better supports to put them on, smoother printing paper, lenses of more particular and varied applications. No handbooks came with their cameras, as Carlton's did with Smith's, to advise them on "Length of Exposure" or "Duration of Development." Amateurs were often their own chemists. They had to learn from experience, to record success and to study failure. How did the time of day and the clarity of the atmosphere advance or retard their work? What lens gave the deepest view of a landscape, and which gave the most just portrait? How could they keep their photographs from fading away?

These were among the questions that were experimentally answered; the solutions were always provisional, for there was always a better way. Each amateur found his own best way, and many were quick to share their secrets. All over the world, from London to Calcutta, from Paris to Philadelphia, they formed societies and published journals. The journals of the 1850s and 1860s are enlivened by the persistence and the quickness of their exchanges — quaint interests they seem in these instamatic times. The pages of *The Photographic Journal* of London and *The Philadelphia Photographer* are full of published secrets: Mr. Goddard's communication to the members of the Royal Photographic Society on the "Self-registering Sun-dial;" Mr. Hislop's many paragraphs titled "A Word for Sugar in the Iron Developer"; and "Albumenizer's" solution to the problem of "Discoloration of Albumen Paper." All of these people were avidly making photographs, and if the names Goddard and Hislop do not conjure up their pictures, it is not for their want of enthusiastic attention to the art-science that aroused their devotion. "Spent the day in attempting to photograph, but the chemicals refused to work properly," wrote the amateur Lewis Carroll in 1858. He was not daunted by the difficulties, however; that was the year in which he exhibited five photographs in the London Society's Annual Exhibition.

Yet it *is* amazing, considering the finicky wet-collodion processing, that there were so many amateurs early in the third quarter of the nineteenth century. But that process itself, introduced in 1851, extended the practice of photography beyond the confinements of the unique Daguerreotype and the restrictions on use that Talbot had imposed on his invention. The Great Exhibition of All the World's Trades, held in London in 1851, provided a forum for information and a focal point for royal praise (Queen Victoria was especially enchanted by the stereoscopic photographs); it was also a strong stimulant. The wet-collodion process promised shorter exposure times, making portraiture more possible, and produced a negative from which many copies could be made. Albumen paper, made with the white of eggs, overcame the general objection to Talbot's coarse-appearing positive of sensitized drawing paper and provided tonal gradation as beautifully smooth as those of a Daguerreotype. The practice of photography increased so noticably that, in 1862, on the occasion of another international exposition, the *Times* of London declared, "Photography may be said to be in an entirely new class since 1851; indeed, the art itself can scarcely be said to have existed at that time, if we compare it with its now universal spread."

Still, it was an art to be practised only by the most determined amateurs, like Carroll, and that determination was necessarily accompanied by means. Cameras were individually made of finely finished wood, bird's eye maple, mahogany or cherry; Lewis Carroll's fictional photographer "Hiawatha" had one made of rosewood, "made of sliding, folding rosewood." The fittings were brass, and the lenses specially ground. These, the glass plates, the developing and printing apparatus, and even the room in which the dark processes were performed did not come cheap. The members of the Amateur Photographic Association of London, who often met in a home on Portsmouth Square, included a number of titled and otherwise distinguished names. It seems odd today to picture the Viscountess Jocelyn or Colonel, the Hon. Dudley Fitzgerald de Ros, former equerry to the Prince Consort, holding the corners of their glass plates firmly between thumb and forefinger while flowing the sticky iodized collodion evenly over the surfaces, or, subsequently, varnishing the developed plates, taking care to avoid blisters or cracks. That, however, is what had to be done by most amateurs in the wet-collodion era.

"I am quite sure about Mrs. Cameron's photographs," wrote Ann Thackeray Ritchie to a friend. "She paddles in cold water till two o'clock every morning." Did those other amateurs do as Mrs. Cameron had done in 1863, efface their first picture by rubbing their hands over the filmy side of the glass? Probably, but, like her, they persevered. By 1869, Mr. Glaisher, secretary to the London Amateur Association, could report "the steadily increasing prosperity of the Association, and the great increase in the number of pictures of sufficient excellence" contributed for discussion and exhibition by its members — 766 in that year.

In the days before panchromatic film and prepared solutions, the photographic journals extended help to amateurs in their correspondence columns:

To the Amateur — The joke in *Punch* of the flour-dredger, is, no doubt, occasionally a reality. In our early days of photographic experiment, we remember dusting over a gentleman's florid whiskers (they were red, which would turn out black in the print), much to his horror, in order to approach reality.

To the Amateur — The blue glass for the operating room we believe to be needless.

———. We have mislaid your exact address. The whole picture is good, but the color of the white portion of the paper is not sufficiently kept; probably the negative is a little underexposed. An *over*-exposed negative prints well if the transparent portions are cleaned by a weak iodine solution before you proceed to intensify.

Note — Chloride of lime lying about the darkroom will cause pin-holes in negatives.

Such were the problems that faced Viscountess Jocelyn and Lord de Ros; they were also the concerns of American amateurs. Outstanding among them were the engineer Coleman Sellers of Philadelphia, inventor of the Kinematoscope and later developer of hydroelectric power at Niagara, and the patrician Fairman Rogers, whose four-in-hand was painted by Thomas Eakins and who wrote on the uses to which Muybridge's first motion studies might be put. The difficulties of photography in that era attracted people with exceptional experimental skills.

Although amateur activity in this country lagged somewhat behind activity in Great Britain, by 1864, the year in which *The Philadelphia Photographer,* journal of that city's Amateur Society, was first issued, there had been such a growth of interest that *The Scientific American* could recommend photography as a fashionable hobby for young people and for ladies. "Photography," said the editor, "is by no means as difficult or laborious as ordinary needlework." This sounds like a statement by someone who has done neither. Compare the ease with which the young lady of fashion might sit by the fire plying her needle over the embroidery frame with the messy and arduous process of coating, sensitizing, exposing and developing the wet-collodion plate, and doing it all in about fifteen minutes, before the plate dried and became useless. The portable dark tents used on the landscape expeditions that amateurs so enjoyed, and the barrows in which the bottles of chemicals and other necessary gear were trundled to the selected view didn't mix with the requirements of 1860s fashion, and eventually only the fanatic persisted.

It was the amateur's need to free himself from the wet plate and the dark tent, from all the cumbersome traps that accompanied a wet-collodion excursion, that led to the development of the dry plate. Along with the dry plate came cameras that had been especially developed to accomodate its greater sensitivity. These advancements initiated the era that continues today, a period in which the practice of photography is not limited to amateurs of privilege, but in which photography is literally popular. Albert Lichtwark, the progressive director of the Hamburg Kunsthalle, recognized this in 1893, when he organized an exhibition of 6,000 photographs by amateurs. He called it *The Peoples' Art.*

Amateurs took the lead in the attempts made to preserve the sensitized collodion so it did not have to be developed while still moist. As Helmut and Alison Gernsheim note in their 1955 *History of Photography,* the preservatives tried suggest the inventory of a pantry shelf — sugar, honey, caramel, malt, raspberry and raisin syrups, sherry, beer, vinegar, skimmed milk, tea and

14

licorice, among other culinary staples. It is nice to note, for those who like dark Italian roast, that it was Ottavio Baratti, editor of the Italian journal *La Camera Oscura,* who in 1867 proposed the "Coffee Dry Process":

Preservative Solution
Water .... 300 grams
Ground Coffee 130
Refined Sugar 15

While journals on each side of the Atlantic were full of proposals for one preservative or another, amateurs in England in the 1870s were giving up on trying to preserve the collodion and were turning to gelatin emulsions. They so successfully developed a gelatin-bromide emulsion that glass plates coated with it and used dry were being commercially manufactured before the end of the decade. These experimentors followed the immediate lead of the physician Dr. Richard Leach Maddox, who published his formula in 1871. Maddox's dry plates, however, were much less sensitive than wet-collodion plates and were difficult to develop. Within a decade, though, gelatin-bromide dry plates had been made that were almost twice as sensitive as those of the wet process. Amateurs welcomed their use. Professionals, with their studio setups and their stables of darkroom operators, had to be persuaded to use the new method. Still, by 1882, the Gernsheims note, only one-and-a-half percent of the almost 1,500 prints hung in the London Photographic Society's annual exhibition were printed from wet-collodion negatives; the rest were made from dry-plate negatives. "With these plates, photography becomes almost a child's toy," said the Archbishop of York, himself the president of The Dry Plate Club since its founding in 1872. A professional, on the other hand, called the spread of the use of dry plates "humbug," a passing fad devised for amateurs.

The names of the English photographers who contributed to the revolutionary development of the dry plate — Maddox, Harrison, Burgess and Kennett — are known to specialists; the name of one of the first American manufacturers, George Eastman, has become universally known. W.F. Carlton may have had Eastman in mind when he called photography "almost entirely the product of amateur effort and experiment."

George Eastman, a bank clerk in Rochester, New York, became an amateur photographer in 1877. Robert Taft tells the story of his beginnings in *Photography and the American Scene.* Eastman was planning a trip to Santo Domingo, a possible place to invest his savings, and took the suggestion of a colleague who had worked with the Powell Survey of the American West earlier in the decade that he photograph what he saw there. He bought a wet-plate camera and accessories, and took lessons from a local professional. The trip was put off, but Eastman kept at his new hobby. On his first photographic excursion he packed a leaky bottle of the necessary silver bath in the trunk that held his clothes. He was a fastidious man; the irremediable staining of all his apparel strongly impressed him with the need for portable dry plates. By now

Eastman's interest in photography had extended to the reading of photographic journals, and he found in *The British Journal of Photography* a formula for gelatin-bromide dry plates. By 1879, while still clerking in the bank, he was selling plates made from his modification of Bennett's formula to the professional who had originally taught him the wet-collodion process. A year later he was selling them through a commercial photographic supply house, and by 1882 he was no longer a bank clerk, but president of the company that still carries his name.

These more sensitive plates spurred the manufacture of cameras that would accommodate their speed. Smaller cameras were produced, designed especially for amateurs. In 1879, the earliest American manufacturer of dry plates, Albert Levy, of New York, offered a camera and lens for 4 by 5-inch glass plates with a half-dozen plates, developer, pyro, hypo and "full instructions for working the same" for $12 (multiply this by at least ten for today's cost). Another manufacturer followed with "Cameras for the Millions," and another with one "for amateur photographers, college boys and artists," a group that seems to cut across class and professional lines. One manufacturer announced, as though it were news, that "a large and intelligent class of amateur photographers had made its appearance." How must the Philadelphia amateurs of two decades earlier, Coleman Sellers and Fairman Rogers, have taken that? William H. Walker, founder of the Rochester Optical Company, later the manufacturer of Harry Smith's camera, offered a camera, kit and instruction manual for $10, and an additional

camera free to anyone who would form a camera club. Walker advertised, as Eastman would later, in a popular journal, *The Century Magazine*, rather than exclusively in photographic journals, as the earlier custom had been. One of his ads for Walker's Pocket Camera is reprinted in Eaton S. Lathrop, Jr.'s *A Century of Cameras*.

Photography Made Easy for Everybody

By the use of Walker's Pocket Camera and Complete Dry Plate Outfits, with full instructions furnished, anybody absolutely without experience in photography may take as fine photographic views as a professional photographer. An entirely new, instructive and delightful pastime. Invaluable for tourists.

Or the tourist might prefer something larger, the "Tourograph", a dry-plate view camera packed for travel. For amateurs more on the run, there was a range of "detective" cameras, smaller and lighter cameras that could be concealed — the French *Photo-Revolver de Poche* of 1883, which epitomized that wicked expression, "to shoot a picture;" The Instantograph of 1884; and the Concealed Vest Camera, introduced in October 1886, "18,000 sold by December 1890," said the ads for it. It was not recommended for the obese. "The only view would be of the sky," an observer noted. Cameras were also fitted into hats, made to look like books and disguised as binoculars.

In 1888, the prudent George Eastman, realizing that "in order to make a large business, we would have to reach a large public," brought out "an improved detective camera, a film camera, the role holder integral to it." This was the first Kodak. The camera held a roll of film on a flexible base, and the amateur could choose, if he wished, to have the difficult stripping process and subsequent development of the film done at the factory. "You press the button, we do the rest," was Eastman's catchy slogan. "Anybody who can wind a watch can use the Kodak camera." Following the exposure of 100 negatives, the amateur could go to the post office rather than into the darkroom, mail the camera and $10 to the Eastman Dry Plate & Film Company in Rochester and, in time, receive from there his reloaded camera and his prints and negatives. The circular image offered a compositional advantage to the amateur, who could take his main subject in the center of the circle and let the edges go. By 1889, when the Kodak I, with its transparent, flexible film appeared, the processing might more easily be done at home; but the elegantly dressed women in a Kodak advertisement probably preferred to send the film out. Darkroom work doesn't seem to be in their future as they chorus to a demure salesgirl, hands folded behind her back, "Oh! Isn't it lovely! I must have a Kodak!"

Amateurs were now equipped to take photographs that were both instantaneous and candid. F.C. Beach surveyed the decade or so of "Modern Amateur Photography," that is, of dry-plate photography, in *Harper's Monthly* for May 1888. Beach's modern amateur was no show-off. He felt a certain reticence in taking a picture in a crowd, a reticence that could not have been felt in the era of the conspicuous wet-plate camera, and one that is not particularly observable today, however miniature the instrument. The amateur, Beach said, felt more comfortable, less caught-in-the-act, with the small, detective-type camera, the button or the vest camera, for instance. "In taking a picture, it is only necessary to walk up to within a few feet of the object, then to quickly pull the string; a slight sound or click at once apprises the operator that the picture is taken." The "operator" could then retreat, presumably undetected.

How did all this ease and speed affect the modern amateur? It offered a new class of subject, one that did not sit still. The subject being everything to an amateur, this expansion of the range of possibilities greatly enhanced the already evident attractions of photography as a hobby, and increased the number of participants. The act of taking a photograph, and of having a photograph taken, became a much less unusual occurence. To be the subject of a photograph became a part of modern life; there was nothing solemn, strange or celebratory about it. The result was a portrayal in photographs of life as it was being lived, of common as well as uncommon events, as Carlton called them, events in which everyone participated. The amateur photographer not only observed but recorded them. Among the now-possible subjects mentioned by the American writer and amateur photographer Alexander Black were "fragments of street scenery, little genre bits in out-of-the-way corners, tableaux in rustic or town life, requiring instant capture." It was Black who called the dry plate "the keynote of amateur photography" in an article published in *The Century* in 1887 and reprinted in Beaumont Newhall's 1981 book *Photography: Essays & Images.* "In the open air," said Black, "nothing is closed against the 'detective,'" with its exposure of 1/200th of a second, the wink of an eye.

When the fine British amateur, Lady Hawarden, took a picture in the early 1860s titled *Girl Skipping Rope*, she was really taking a picture of a girl who might skip rope. The rope was in the girl's hands and she looked ready to skip, but any skipping she might do had to be done before or after that photograph was taken. A motion as quick as skipping could not then be photographed. But in the 1880s, two and a half decades later, the snippet of time that amateurs might take from their daily lives included divers diving, jugglers juggling, trains chugging, bands marching and girls skipping. All of these actions, and more like them were added to their repertory of photographic subjects — the customary portraits, still-lifes, landscapes and architectural views — by amateurs who had recently become equipped with faster plates and lighter, hand-held cameras.

Among these amateur photographers was Alfred Stieglitz. As a student in Berlin in his early twenties, he was one of those college boys to whom a camera manufacturer had advertised; but he was a college boy with a difference in regard to photography. He studied at the Berlin Polytechnic with Wilhelm H. Vogel, professor of optics and photochemistry, a man superbly in command of all the technical and artistic problems and possibilities that the recent revolution in photography had presented. For twenty years Vogel had been the critic and general correspondent from Berlin for such journals as *The Philadelphia Photographer* and had made the initial discovery that led to the manufacture of orthochromatic emulsions and, later, of color film. Stieglitz profited from his teacher's technical and critical experience and became adept at the most difficult subjects — those taken in snow and rain, with clouds and steam in the air, in shadow penetrated by shafts of brilliant light, of people gesturing, unposed, in the street.

After a vacation jaunt through Italy in 1887, Stieglitz entered twelve photographs in a contest sponsored by the British journal *The Amateur Photographer.* "Holiday Work" was the theme, a theme that implied avocation. Peter Henry Emerson, the most famous of Britain's 15,000 amateurs, widely known for his challenge to the artificiality and stiffness that had become increasingly evident in the work shown in photographic salons, judged the competition. He called Stieglitz' photographs the "only spontaneous work in the whole collection," and awarded his *A Good Joke* the first prize. In New York and in Paris during the 1890s and early 1900s, Stieglitz continued to attempt difficult subjects, ones requiring the canniest use of the fast, hand-held camera: *The Terminal; A Wet Day on the Boulevard; Winter, Fifth Avenue.* A description of any of them must use an active verb: steaming, raining, snowing.

It is curious that Stieglitz, who devoted his own holiday work to the most active and present moments, became the inventor, so to speak, and the leader of that group of photographers who forsook vivacity for timelessness. In the late 1800s and early years of this century he gathered this group about him and eventually gave it a name, "The Photo-Secession;" a journal, *Camera Work;* and a gallery, The Little Galleries of the Photo-Secession. In defining his goal to have photography recognized as a fine art, Stieglitz emphasized through the Photo-Secession group a kind of photography called *pictorial;* that is, derived from pictures that were accepted as fine art, from paintings, drawings and prints in traditional media. Pictorial photographs were treated to artistic manipulation; they showed gummed brush-strokes, drawn lines and etched-out whites. Many of the pictorialists started as painters, and their photographs sometimes could not be differentiated from prints in non-photographic media. The Japanese influence, suggested by Whistler, became part of the pictorial photographer's style, and Whistler's own tonalities, his vaporizing light, were sought in pictorial photographs. Largely through Stieglitz' promotion of it, this sort of photography overcame resistance to photography in museums of fine art throughout the world. This success of his brainchild was for a while gratifying to him, but one senses Stieglitz' falling out of love with pictorial photography, a disenchantment that was accompanied by his growing interest in the avant-garde art of Europe and America. As he felt the modern urgency of that art, of Picasso, Brancusi, Matisse and Hartley, he consigned pictorialism to photography's past. He came to the conclusion in 1908

that "Photography cannot be pictorial any more than can music or oratory. Photography is photography, neither more nor less." As for his own photographs, he described them as "snapshots, nothing more, nothing less; but carefully studied ones."

The world of pictorial photography is a world Harry Smith might have entered when he started photographing in 1900. He might have joined the California Camera Club, the largest amateur organization in the West, whose offices were on Market Street in San Francisco. There, he might have learned to print in platinum, the preferred paper for artful photographs, and he might have shown in the club's salons. But he did not. Guided by Carlton, he maintained a photographic innocence that recalled pre-Secessionist times. Carlton, and Smith, too, went this far and no farther: "The man having the eye of an artist, who knows how to seek the best position, will at all times give the best picture." Harry Smith was successful at it and remained content with photography, nothing more and nothing less.

The verb Carlton uses in the statement is interesting, "give," not "get." Amateur photographers do seem to give something to their subjects; a sense of their individuality and an exactitude of the time and place in which they exist. Wright Morris calls this quality *authenticity* in his marvelous recent essay "Photographs, Images and Words." A certain line between amateur and high-art photography is passed when the subject is not so much itself as it is a form in a photograph. At a recent symposium, Charis Wilson, Edward Weston's wife and model, was asked, to the embarrassment of some in the audience, how she felt when she looked at the photographs Weston had taken of her naked in the dunes of Oceāno, California. "I have never thought of them as pictures of myself," she said. "I always thought of them as Edward's wonderful photographs." While it is our gain, something is lost (to use Morris' terms) in Weston's nudes that is not lost, for instance, in E.J. Bellocq's photographs of the naked inhabitants of Storyville in New Orleans.

Here is another paradox. Harry Smith did not take photographs of the people in his life for us to look at. He took pictures of his family and friends for them to look at; they were shared mementoes of a personal life. He mounted them in albums and on cards, studying and checking emphatically Carlton's directions to "place the print carefully on the card mount, working from the center to the ends so as to be free from air bubbles." He could not have dreamed that we today, with our appetite for looking at photographs whetted by all the exhibitions and publications of the past several decades, would take his photographs away from the family context and see in them purely photographic qualities. It baffles his daughter, who says of them, "They're just photographs." In the background we hear the echo of Stieglitz' "and nothing less." Among the qualities that attract us in Smith's photographs are the immediacy that is also found in quick drawings from life; the quality of light on certain fabrics available otherwise in a sort of painting that is no longer practised; and the direct, essentially photographic,

way in which he approached his subjects, a way that lets us see them as he saw them and as, we must believe, they really were.

A young photographer who showed her mother pictures she had taken in a city street got this response: "Why would you take a picture of someone you don't know?" Today, however, many of us look with interest at photographs of people we don't know. Our fascination is in the photograph, not in the people. And here there is a further twist. When the people are presented with candor and close feeling, as they are in Harry Smith's photographs, when they are not overridden with photographic style, we want to know as much as we can about the subjects. Biography as well as photography is a modern passion.

What we find, led by Harry Smith's photographs, is the story of a simple but difficult life. Harry was born to Danish parents in San Francisco in 1883. His mother had six children; two girls died in infancy, and two boys in their youth. Harry wore a black armband at his wedding, in memory of his brother Eddy, Stephen White reports, having seen the picture in the album, and he memorialized his brother George in the photograph *George at Rest*. What a truly decisive moment that was for him and his family. The family lived in what is called the Mission District of the city, an area of good weather, protected by hills, in which the Franciscan fathers established their Mission in 1776. The phrase "out in the Mission" recognizes that areas' distance from the earlier residential and commercial core of the city. Not too long before San

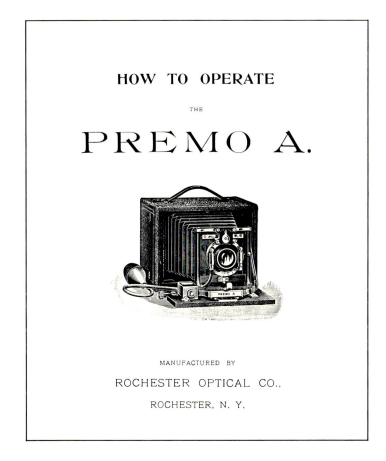

HOW TO OPERATE

THE

PREMO A.

MANUFACTURED BY

ROCHESTER OPTICAL CO.,

ROCHESTER, N. Y.

Francisco's Scandinavian community moved into the substantial homes built there in the 1870s and 1880s and made the Mission District their center, the area was reached by a planked toll road. Even though his father

was a successful businessman, Harry Smith's life had a very small compass. Most of it was conducted within a square half-mile of where he lived. His sweetheart, Agnes Andersen, lived a few blocks away from his family's house; to get to school, he turned the corner on Howard Street and walked for a block and a half.

Occasionally Harry must have gone to his father's ship chandlery near the northern waterfront, and when he started work as a sailmaker in 1905 he traveled there again, for the loft where he worked was off East Street, as that part of what is now the Embarcadero was called. He did get on the Howard Street trolley, which, for a nickel, took him and his camera to Golden Gate Park, or to Ocean Beach and the Cliff House, and on occasion he went to central Market Street. Excursions to the country in the summer took him out of this orbit when he went to visit the summer camps and ranches of Danish friends and relatives, his neighbors in the city. There, when he was fourteen, he met Agnes, his future wife; they honeymooned in 1907 at a resort near these ranches. After his marriage he moved a few doors away from the house in which he had been brought up, and later to a three-story house a few blocks away that he and Agnes shared with his parents and his remaining brother's family. Harry Smith died in 1973 in a Danish old peoples' home.

He had always been handy, but with an increasing deafness that started in his youth, he gave up his musical hobby, playing the cornet, and turned more to his silent hobby, photography. Deafness isolated him, as it always does; perhaps that is why he didn't join the Camera Club.

Nevertheless, he was what was called then "an enthusiastic amateur." His Premo A, a folding-bed, collapsible-bellows camera of a type first made in 1883, used 4 by 5-inch dry plates, a respectable size for the serious amateur. He had his own darkroom, where he developed his plates and then printed them on Aristotype, a shiny, brown-toned printing-out-paper that Eugene Atget also used. For some indoor photographs he used the tricky magnesium flash, and often put himself in the picture by using the Premo's extended bulb release.

Harry's enthusiasm led him to photograph difficult subjects such as buildings lighted at night and bathers by a light-reflecting river. He could use his camera for instantaneous work, snapshots, as well as for longer exposures. Had there been a snowstorm in San Francisco, he would have been out in it with his Premo A. The night photographs, among his first pictures, show how well he mastered his new hobby. They were possibly suggested to him by the fame of the photographs taken at night of the lighted buildings of California's 1894 Mid-Winter Fair. Of the electrical illumination of Sunset City, as the fair grounds were called, the San Francisco *Examiner* had said, "it is regarded as the most beautiful sight at the Fair," which included such sights as an Esquimaux Village, a Japanese Tea Garden (still a beautiful attraction in Golden Gate Park) and a Temple of Oranges. When I.W. Taber, the Fair's official photographer, published his photograph of Sunset City illuminated by 3,213 incandescent lamps, the *Examiner* said, "The photograph of the scene is as great an achievement as the illumination

it pictures. All similar attempts at Chicago (in 1893, at the World's Columbian Exposition) to photograph electric illuminations were failures. This, therefore, is deemed to be the best photograph of the kind ever taken." Taber's exposure in 1894 took thirty minutes; Harry Smith used a smaller camera in 1900, and his exposure was one-fifteenth of that. The result must have felt like a triumph to him. In successfully recording the gorgeous illumination he was entering his own contest and winning.

The photographs he took of San Francisco while the city burned and still trembled during those three days in April 1906 are also of special interest, both photographically and historically. Harry Smith's house shook at 5:13 a.m. on April 18th, but it did not burn as much of the city did when broken gas jets burst into flames. He must have grabbed his camera as soon as he could and rushed over to Agnes's house to see if the Andersen family was all right. Assured of that, he turned down Valencia Street, just a few blocks away, and saw what remained of the four-story Valencia Street Hotel. What a sight! Did he know then that forty of the five-hundred people who died in the earthquake were entombed there? Throughout the 18th and 19th of April, 1906, when everyone believed that San Francisco was doomed to total destruction and it was reported that "a great fire is raging in the Mission District, and is entirely out of control," it took a strong pull from the camera to keep Harry Smith out in the streets photographing. No doubt he sensed the magnitude of the disaster, one that has been compared with the eruption of Vesuvius and the destruction of Pompeii; and he felt that, no matter what, he had to get pictures of it. Perhaps, with his keen eye, he recognized the transforming, even picturesque quality of those fire-wrought ruins, in which "structural atrocities" became ruins of classical dignity, our own Acropolis and Parthenon, as Louis J. Stellman wrote in *The Vanished Ruin Era.*

Harry Smith's earthquake photographs mirror the event and rise to it; they are extraordinary, as it was. Photographs such as that of the family cat might have been anticipated. Family dogs, their eyes a milky blur, appear even in amateur daguerreotypes. Between these two extremes, the public event and the private pleasure, Harry Smith produced a range of compellingly beautiful and revealing photographs. There are intimate portraits of his father's light-struck face, with broad planes shown against the intricate crabbiness of the patterned wallpaper, a photograph that Vuillard or Degas might have taken; portraits of Agnes in her ruffles and smocked gown, all sunshine and smiles under the dark shadow of her wide ribboned hat; of the hilarious little boys with big ears; of his stern parents' dark selves glimpsed through the lights and fantastic tracery of the oddly embellished Danish Christmas tree. And one cannot count on finding, even in the most enthusiastic amateur's work, the satisfaction derived from discovering all the furnishings of all the rooms — the improvised tent, their vacation home with its Samuel Soda chest and bouquet of black-eyed Susans; the parlor's calla lilies, the sail loft's "Red Mike, Ex-Pugilist," to say nothing of the sailmakers, one of them with a knobby knee showing through the hole in his jeans. There is alot to look at in photographs like these, much that provides a complicated sort of pleasure. This pleasure is a photographic pleasure.

Every amateur has a range of subjects that are congruent with his life. Harry Smith's life, lived as it was, will not give us the elegantly bold images of wealth that came out of Jacques Henri Lartigue's boyhood, or the royal stateliness and ceremony that Maria Feyodorovna, the mother of Tzar Nicholas II, caught with her panoramic camera and pasted in her family albums, or the dry toughness recorded by Christian Bathelmess, an Army officer on the Montana plains. This is self-evident. But through the thoroughness of their revelations they will, like any photographs taken for the love of recording the common and uncommon events in a life, invite our delighted, amused and sometimes amazed participation.

This very human desire to see representations of subjects that could not otherwise be seen, time or distance making it impossible, was the initial attraction of photography. Similarly, the present universal interest in the medium can be partially attributed to the non-objective painting of the middle of this century. Today, when many photographers seem to be foresaking objectivity in favor of interior fantasies achieved by marking, embroidering, collaging or otherwise manipulating the photograph, simply photographic photographs such as Harry A. Smith's seem to me a welcome refreshment of the art.

HARRY SMITH: *MAGIC MOMENTS*

PLATE 1: *In the Hammock, Redwood Canyon, 1900*

This self-portrait of Harry A. Smith standing beside his mother and younger brother is among the earliest of his photographs. The Smith's vacationed near Guerneville, in an area north of San Francisco that was popular with the city's Scandinavian community. At the time this photograph was made Harry Smith was only seventeen. A self-taught photographer, his unusual talent for composition is evident. The bright sun illuminates the sitters and the hammock while the woods behind are hidden in darkness.

PLATE 2: *Tent Interior, Redwood Canyon, 1900.*

A holiday in the country provided the time needed for the young photographer to practice his newly acquired interest. This interior study of the makeshift tent he shared with his family shows the somewhat haphazard arrangement of the cooking area. Supplies had to be carried from home, a difficult task in the days before the wide-spread use of the automobile and the manufacture of light-weight camping equipment. While the photograph shows the primitive conditions in which the family lived, it also suggests the peace and beauty that existed at the isolated site.

PLATE 3: *Around the Camp Table, Redwood Canyon, 1900*

The bright noonday sun illuminated the background as Harry Smith photographed his family and their friends after a shared lunch. The adults for the most part look irritated by the photographer's interruption of their conversation, while the children couldn't keep still long enough for Harry to make his exposure.

PLATE 4: *Rescue Boats Off Ocean Beach, c. 1900*

The Life Saving Station at the Northwest corner of San Francisco's Golden Gate Park provided part of the attraction of this area. Swimming and boating were popular recreations at Ocean Beach and the public was invited to watch the lifesaving boats as they practiced. It is a sign of Harry Smith's ability to use his camera well that, even in this early exposure, he took his picture at the moment the lead boat rode the final wave into shore. Whether this was a training session or a real rescue is left to the imagination.

PLATE 5: *The Cliff House from Ocean Beach, before 1907*

A landmark for San Francisco residents and visitors since the mid-1850s, the Cliff House was twice destroyed by fire before the one photographed by Harry Smith was built in the 1890s. In 1907 it also met the fate of its predecessors and another Cliff House, not nearly as beautiful, was built on the same spot. It still stands today. Photographed looking north, the hill to the right is Sutro Heights; the beach below is Ocean Beach. The pier carried a pipe used to pump ocean water to various salt water baths that were popular in the city at the time. The cliff house was a favorite subject for photographers throughout the late 19th century. Professionals usually photographed it straight on, or from Sutro Heights. By using the wind-blown dune grasses for his foreground, Harry Smith changed the scale of the landmark, giving it a doll house-like appearance.

PLATE 6: *Glasshouse, Sutro Heights, c. 1900*

Sutro Heights was a popular recreation area for San Francisco residents. The nearby Sutro Baths were a famous feature, and the gardens, where Harry Smith's photograph of this greenhouse was made, were open to the public. Though an important part of the city's tradition, the Sutro Baths were destroyed in the 1960s; the proposed development of the area has not occurred.

PLATE 7: *The Chronicle and Examiner Buildings, September 9, 1900*

California gained admission to the Union on September 9, 1850. For this fiftieth anniversary of the event, both Market Street and the buildings along it were decorated with lights. Taken in the early evening — the clock reads approximately 7:25 — this difficult night exposure must have proved a challenge to the seventeen-year-old photographer. The blurred hand on the clock shows that the exposure took several minutes. The wind may have moved the lighted decorations, giving them a blurred quality as well. The Examiner Building is to the right, the bright light comes from a sign spelling out its name. The Chronicle Building is on the left. The *Examiner* and the *Chronicle*, along with the *Call*, were the three major newspapers in San Francisco at the time; their offices were all located at the intersection of Third, Geary and Kearney Streets. In the great fires that followed the 1906 earthquake the Examiner Building was leveled. The Chronicle clock tower was destroyed and the building itself gutted by the flames.

PLATE 8: *The Chronicle Building, September 9, 1900.*

The activities of the Admission Day celebration can be seen along Market Street to the left of the photograph. In the street itself is a large California State Flag. The office lights in the Chronicle Building have been turned off and the dates 1850 and 1900 are illuminated on the two sides visible in the photograph.

PLATE 9: *Temple of Music, Golden Gate Park, c. 1900*

This popular landmark was built for the city by sugar manufacturer Adolph Spreckels at a cost of $75,000. At the time Harry Smith took this photograph free concerts were given by a 50-piece band on Sundays and public holidays. The outdoor seating could hold 20,000 people and was shaded by specially planted elm and maple trees. The Temple of Music was built of Colusa sandstone. It received severe damage in the 1906 earthquake, but still remained in use. In June of that year the commencement exercises for the public schools were held there. The damage was repaired and the Temple of Music still stands in Golden Gate Park.

PLATE 10: *3071 24th Street, San Francisco, c. 1902*

Not only did Harry Smith photograph public monuments in San Francisco such as the Cliff House and the Temple of Music, he photographed buildings in his own neighborhood. His father, Henry Smith, owned several pieces of property in the Danish community around Howard (now South Van Ness) and Dolores Streets. This vacant building with the "to let" signs in the upper windows might have been one of those properties.

The young photographer had only to step out on the third story balcony of his house (see Plate 12) in order to photograph the houses across the street. The fires after the 1906 earthquake did not burn as far as this area and most of this neighborhood survived intact.

PLATE 12: *The Smith House on Howard Street, c. 1902*

The Smith family moved to 2616 Howard Street when Harry Smith was thirteen years old. They lived in this house until 1909, when they moved just a few doors away. Most of the homes in this area were built in the 1870s and 1880s, as the city expanded from its earlier center to the north.

PLATE 13: *Self-Portrait in the Backyard, c. 1902*

The well-balanced symmetry of this photograph provides force to Harry Smith's self-portrait, which he took behind his Howard Street home when he was about twenty years old. The end of the cord that passes from the bushes at the left and over the gate is hidden from view in his hand, allowing him to snap the shutter at any moment he wished.

PLATE 14: *Catherine Smith and a Friend Sewing, c. 1904*

Catherine Smith's maiden name was Hansen; like her husband she emigrated from Denmark to San Francisco. She appears in several of her son's photographs and never manages to smile for him. On the right in this photograph, the light from the window illuminates what seems to be an expression of pain on her face. Mrs. Smith had six children, including two daughters who died in infancy and two boys who were to die before their teens. Only Harry and his brother Walter reached maturity.

PLATE 15: *The Celebration, c. 1904*

Harry Smith photographed one of his younger brothers with his friend during the celebration of a birthday or some other event. Each boy had been carefully scrubbed and dressed for the occasion. The Smith family enjoyed music and several of the boys played instruments. Harry's specialty was the cornet.

PLATE 16: *The Smith Family Cat*

It may have been the way the afternoon sun hit the fur of the cat that motivated Harry Smith to set up his camera for this photograph. To darken the background he draped a fabric behind the chair. While setting up the shot he may have made too much noise, waking the cat and causing this condescending look from his unsuspecting subject.

PLATE 17: *Ellen and the Andersen Boys, c. 1903*

Harry Smith met his future wife, Agnes Andersen, on a camping trip with his family around the year 1900, when he was just beginning to photograph. Her parents were active in the Danish Church and her family lived close to the Smiths in San Francisco. This photograph may have been taken at the Andersen home. It shows Agnes' younger sister, Ellen, in the center with her two brothers, Walter at the far left, and Arthur at the right. The boy directly to Ellen's left is one of Harry's younger brothers, possibly Eddy.

PLATE 18: *Self-Portrait with Dog, Oaklane Ranch, 1904*

The Smiths visited the Hansens, possibly relatives of Harry's mother, in the summer of 1904 on their ranch in Dry Creek Valley, north of San Francisco and not far from the town of Glen Ellen, where the writer Jack London lived. London wrote about the area in the book *Valley of the Moon.* The title was loosely translated from the Indians words *tso noma,* or "earth" and "village". This is a beautiful area rich in farmland and vineyards, and the holiday gave Harry Smith time to work with his camera. He did a number of exceptional images around the Hansen ranch. Accompanied by one of the Hansen's dogs, Harry set up his camera in front of this large oak to portray himself as a typical country bumpkin, a straw dangling from the side of his mouth. The shadow in the right foreground indicates the presence of someone, possibly his younger brother, to snap the shutter for him.

PLATE 19: *Peter Claussen, Oaklane Ranch, 1904*

One of Smith's finest portraits is this of a crusty old Dane who worked on the Hansen family ranch. The newly-cut boards of the structure provide a strong background. Claussen faces the camera fearlessly, the butt of his cigar firmly gripped in his teeth.

PLATE 20: *The Hansens and Claussen at the Oaklane Ranch, 1904*

The occasion of this photograph is not noted. The tangled mass of vines sandwiches the people between the foreground and the woods behind. With Claussen on the right and another old Dane on the left, the photograph has structural balance as well as a rich visual content. Amateurs like Smith felt free to include elements in their pictures that professional photographers might have omitted. By using the vines as a foreground, Smith chose a setting more natural to the ranch environment than one might expect to see.

PLATE 21: *Japanese Workers, Oaklane Ranch, 1904*

Large numbers of Japanese immigrants entered the country around the turn of the century. They worked in factories and fields all along the West Coast. Four of the workers from the Hansen's ranch posed here along with two of Harry Smith's younger brothers, George and possibly Walter.

This photograph combines many of the elements that make Harry Smith's work so successful. The girl at the center breaks the photograph both vertically and horizontally. There is an equal balance in the foreground and the background. The instructions of W.F. Carlton's photographic handbook, which Smith received along with his Premo A camera, are clearly followed here: "Many commonplace scenes require only the proper lighting, and perhaps the introduction of a proper figure in the right place to make it a beautiful subject for the camera. The commonplace is always attractive when well treated."

PLATE 23: *Windmill and Fence, Oaklane Ranch, 1904*

This area of Sonoma County around the Valley of the Moon has been known for the high quality of its vineyards, which can be seen on the hill behind. The miscellaneous clutter of country life dominates the foreground. The windmill plays a key role in centering the image.

PLATE 24: *Haystacks, Oaklane Ranch, 1904*

Haystacks have been popular subjects of both photographers and painters since the early 19th century. Naturalistic photographers such as Peter Henry Emerson and Henry White made important series of pictures of haystacks; they were also used as a motif by the Impressionist painters. Harry Smith chose to photograph the natural curves of the haystacks as they slope down the hill on the Oaklane Ranch. The same path is followed by the fence and the dry creek that runs along it.

PLATE 25: *Fourth of July, Oaklane Ranch, 1904*

Clasping small American flags, the Hansen and Smith families came together for a group portrait. Flags play an important part in many of the photographs Harry Smith made. It is paradoxical that immigrants maintain strong bonds with their own kind in a new country, while asserting a strong loyalty toward their adopted home. Danes have always been fond of the Fourth of July. There is still a large celebration held each year in Denmark on the American Independence Day, with thousands of Danes from all over the country attending.

PLATE 26: *Agnes at Boyes Hot Springs, c. 1904*

Boyes Hot Springs was one of the popular mineral springs, baths and resorts in the area near Sonoma, north of San Francisco. Having met several years earlier, Agnes and Harry may have arranged to meet there to spend a day together, although she was not fond of swimming. In 1904 Agnes had just turned 18, a *femme fatale* sitting with a friend, waiting for the young photographer to record the moment.

PLATE 27: *Jumping in the Pool, Boyes Hot Springs, c. 1904*

Smith's camera captured this celebration of two youths in motion, their bodies lit by the sun, as they jumped from a platform into the warm waters of the mineral springs.

PLATE 28: *Locomotive, c. 1904*

This may have been one of the trains on the California Northwestern line that ran between Sausalito and the resort areas so popular with the San Francisco community. The photograph represents more than the fascination of a young man with the cold black power of the machine. The angle of the photograph and the feeling of motion created in it deal with the important function of the object — to move large groups of people through the hills of Northern California.

PLATE 29: *United Railroad Company Electric Car, Howard Street, after 1902*

Just as the California Northwestern railroads made travel between resort areas and the city relatively simple, the United Railroad Company provided transportation within San Francisco itself. By 1903 there were over 140 miles of electric railroad track to service the city and people could travel anywhere along it for a nickel. The tracks ran along Howard Street, directly in front of Harry Smith's house. With transportation so close at hand he could pack up his photographic gear, get on the streetcar and go easily to almost any area of the city.

PLATE 30: *In the Sail Loft, 46 Clay Street, before April 1906*

Harry Smith attended school only through the sixth grade. It is not known when he began working as a sailmaker, but he is listed in that profession for the first time in 1905. Prior to that he may have served an apprenticeship. The sail loft where he worked was owned by a man named Edward Hendrix. In this photograph of his co-workers, the rolled sails behind them indicate they have just finished an order. That occasion may have provided the excuse for relaxation, play and photography. The sail loft was located close to the waterfront, in an area that was entirely destroyed in one of the fires that closely followed the 1906 earthquake.

PLATE 31: *San Francisco City Hall at Night, c. 1904*

With evenings free after work, the young Harry Smith could roam the city looking for interesting events to photograph. The lighting of public buildings was something of a novelty at the turn of the century, and the initial illumination of the City Hall must have been a major event, judging from the blurred crowd of people and the large number of photographers set up in front of Smith. His long exposure could not catch the moving photographers, but it did record their tripods lined up in a row. Why he chose to move behind them to take the photograph is difficult to say, but the light on the wooden frame buildings along Eighth Street to the right of the picture adds a dimension to Smith's photograph that the photographers standing closer to the City Hall may have failed to include.

PLATE 32: *San Francisco City Hall, after April 18, 1906*

The same building that had been so beautifully illuminated only a short while before, and had taken years to construct, now stands shattered, its frame exposed like that of a skeleton. Harry Smith stood near the place in which he had exposed the night shot; again another photographer stands in front of him to record the scene. Not only was the building itself badly damaged, but the city records were lost along with it.

PLATE 33: *Valencia Street Hotel, April 1906*

The worst disaster during the earthquake itself occurred at this hotel close to where Harry Smith lived. At least forty people were killed here, although the exact count was never known. The hotel was four stories high before the quake. People were trapped in the rubble and many drowned when a broken water main flooded the basement. When Harry Smith took this photograph a day or two after the disaster the water was still flowing on the street in front of the hotel. There were a number of major fires that swept San Francisco following the earthquake; one of these burned this area to the ground.

PLATE 34: *National Iron Works, 1906*

Harry Smith traveled to many parts of the city with his camera to record the disaster caused by the earthquake and fire. This building stood at the corner of Main and Howard, near the waterfront and close to where his father had maintained a ship supply store and saloon. It is not known why he chose to photograph this one remaining structure surrounded by hunks of concrete and two naked chimneys. The man in the horse-drawn wagon appears to be waiting for him. They may have been on the way to the elder Smith's store to check on damage from the earthquake.

PLATE 35: *The Soldier, 1906*

After the earthquake and fire, many troops from nearby Fort Mason and the Presidio, as well as from the California National Guard, were called in to keep order and prevent looting. Often their most difficult job was to force people from their homes and businesses as the fires burned through neighborhood after neighborhood. Smith photographed this recruit in conversation, his rifle casually sitting on his shoulder, while behind him remnants of the ghost city stand in jagged formation.

PLATE 36: *After the Emporium Fire, 1906*

At first the Emporium department store had been spared by the quake. It quickly reopened to sell merchandise to the earthquake victims, but within two days the massive fire that destroyed the three nearby newspaper buildings had gutted the interior of the structure, reducing it to a shell. Smith's camera recorded the damage after the flames died out as well as the feeling of helplessness and frustration of the woman in the foreground. It must have been a feeling shared by all of San Francisco at that moment.

PLATE 37: *The Fire, San Francisco, 1906*

Fires did more damage to San Francisco than did the earthquake itself. Block upon block fell to the raging flames. Firemen without water for their pumps — most of the mains and pipes had broken during the quake — fought as best they could, but often they could only stand by helplessly waiting for the fire to burn itself out. On the left of the picture stand buildings still intact, beside the remains from the destructive fire. People on the street wait and watch, hoping their own homes or businesses would be spared. The electric car wires and the curve of the brick street in the foreground give a rare beauty to a scene of San Francisco in the midst of disaster.

PLATE 38: *Agnes at Cazadero, 1907*

It must have been difficult for the people of San Francisco to see their city in ruins, knowing that only across the Bay life continued at a relatively normal pace. The occasion of Harry Smith and Agnes Andersen's marriage on August 1, 1907, offered the opportunity for them to escape the difficulties of the City for a honeymoon in places they had come to know and love during their childhood. Part of the time was spent in Cazadero, a small resort area some eighty miles north of San Francisco, west of Santa Rosa. Perhaps it was upon their arrival there that Harry chose to take this portrait of his bride beside the tiny station house.

PLATE 39: *Diving at the Russian River, 1907*

Agnes and Harry spent part of their honeymoon at Monte Rio, a resort area along the Russian River not too far from the town of Guerneville. On a warm summer day Harry Smith took out his camera to record the activities along the river.

PLATE 40: *Train at Monte Rio, 1907*

In contrast to the quiet and solitude of Cazadero, Monte Rio was an active and bustling place. It was less than a mile from the famous Bohemian Grove, where the fashionable Bohemian Club of San Francisco held their yearly summer High Jinks. From the size of the crowd at the railroad station it is apparent that a holiday in the country was a popular escape for the tired residents of San Francisco.

PLATE 41: *Agnes in Duboce Park, c. 1908*

Duboce Park is one of the many small parks that exist in San Francisco. After the earthquake the damaged areas were rapidly rebuilt while, at the same time, the city grew into previously unbuilt areas. When Harry brought Agnes here to photograph her a year or two after their marriage, new homes surrounded the park.

PLATE 42: *Harry and Agnes in Duboce Park, c. 1908*

Harry has put himself in the picture again. Dressed in his suit and wearing a bowler hat, possibly to cover his premature baldness, he sits proudly beside his wife. By the time this photograph was taken Smith was having difficulty with his hearing. He had had an illness that resulted in chronic ear problems. An incompetent physician treated him and the treatment eventually caused a nearly total loss of hearing in both ears.

PLATE 43: *Parlor Games #1, c. 1909*

This photograph may have been taken at 2673 Howard Street, where the Smiths lived temporarily. Music figured prominently in their lives until Harry's hearing problems became so bad he could no longer play the cornet. The other couple, their close friends and neighbors, is William and Ida Pow.

PLATE 44: *Parlor Games #2, c. 1909*

Ida and William Pow lived on 18th Street, close to the Smith's. To end an evening of fun they all dressed up for Harry's camera, which recorded this classic scene. Neither the exchange of clothes nor the pipes the women are holding would have been given the social significance they would receive today.

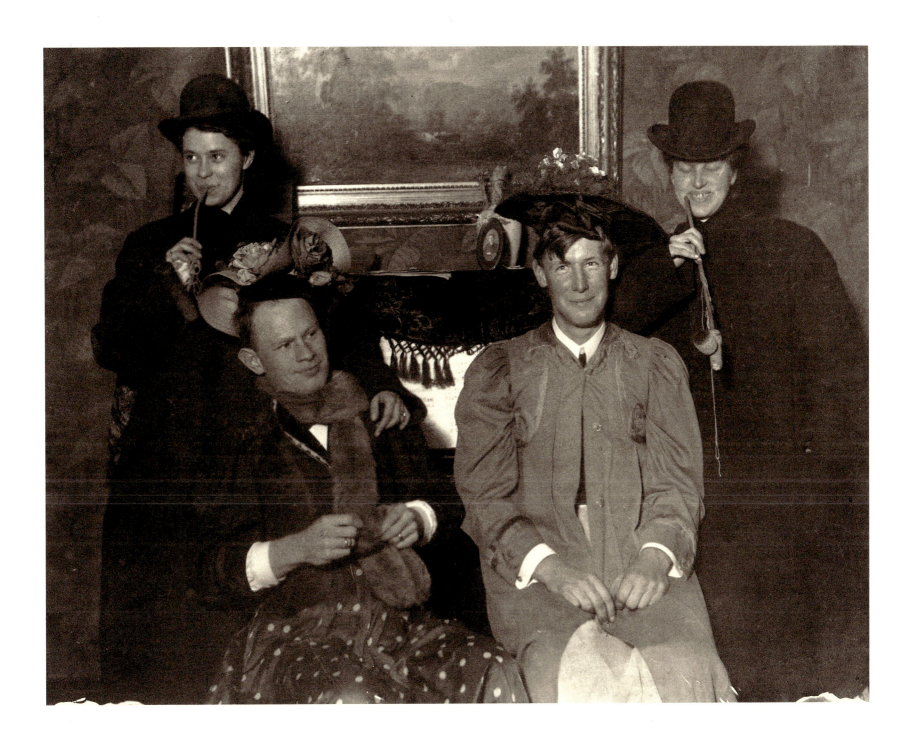

PLATE 45: *Parlor Interior, Dolores Street, c. 1910*

In 1910 Harry and Agnes Smith moved into their own apartment at 1190 Dolores Street, on the second floor of a building Henry Smith had purchased. Henry and his wife, Catherine, moved into the top floor with George, Harry's younger brother. Walter and his family took the apartment on the ground floor. It may have been shortly after Agnes finished decorating their new home that Harry took this photograph of the sunlit parlor. The vase with the deer over the fireplace also appears on top of the piano in plate 43.

PLATE 46: *Ellen and Arthur Andersen with Rover, c. 1910*

While the Smith family experienced much sickness and death among their children, the Andersen children were healthy. This photograph shows Agnes' younger sister, Ellen, and her brother, Arthur. Arthur is the only member of that generation living today. The children's father was a tailor and a highly respected member of the Danish Lutheran Church in San Francisco. As he did with many of his portraits, Harry Smith posed the children facing directly into the sun, against a dark background.

PLATE 47: *George at Rest, c. 1912*

This is one of the most beautiful and painful photographs Harry Smith ever made. Many years earlier he had photographed the coffin of his brother Eddy. The death of another brother, George, left only Walter and Harry among the family's six children. The cause of George's death was believed to be kidney failure. In memory of his brother, Harry and Agnes gave their first child the middle name of Georgia.

PLATE 48: *The Christmas Tree, c. 1912*

The sparse branches are laden with many of the
traditional ornaments of a Danish Christmas. Lighting is
by candle, a practice still continued in Danish homes
today. Popcorn, ornaments, angels and dolls are all placed
on the tree. In the background, Henry and Catherine
Smith sit with their surviving children. The only smile to
be seen is on the face of the doll.

PLATE 49: *Henry Smith, c. 1913*

This sensitive study of Harry's aging father shows the old man with an expression of pain similar to that of his wife in Plate 14. Henry Smith was a successful businessman. He owned property as well as a ship supply store and a saloon on the waterfront. When the earthquake hit a quick-witted assistant loaded all the supplies he could carry into a wagon and brought them to the Smith home. These supplies allowed the Smith family to live well after the earthquake, although Henry retired from business at that time. The wallpaper behind him in this picture hints of a new generation of Smiths, Harry's children; yet the old man seems unable to shake the memories of the past and the losses that caused the family so much suffering.

PLATE 50: *Baby Audrey, c. 1913*

This negative, like a number of others in the Harry Smith collection, has sustained water damage in the years since the picture was taken. These stains, however, often did not create an adverse effect on the quality of the image itself. Audrey was the first child born to Harry and Agnes Smith. Their son, Robert, arrived five years later. Freshly dressed and combed to face the camera, the little girl could not manage to keep her head still for the exposure. She is steadied by her mother as she peers into the camera, the hope of the future.

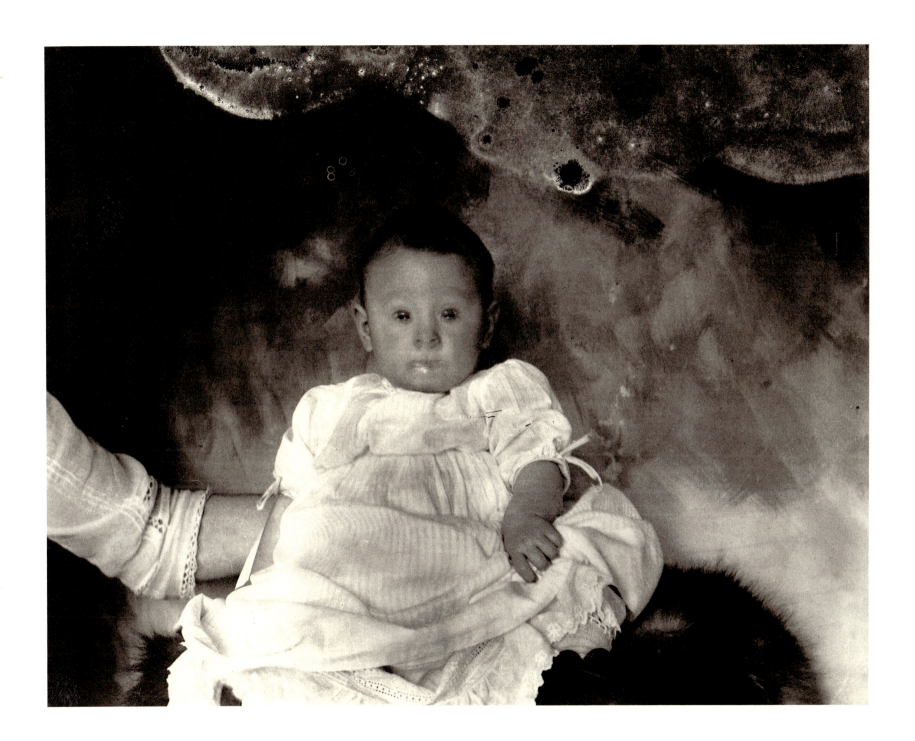

HARRY SMITH PHOTOGRAPHS

In conjunction with the publication of this book, master printer Richard Sullivan has produced archival, high-quality palladium prints from Harry Smith's negatives. Each photograph in the book is available in limited editions of 50 prints each, except for *The Reluctant Child* (frontispiece), which is only available with the limited edition of the book, in an edition of 100. The photographs are approximately 11 by 14 inches, printed on 16 by 20-inch Arches paper. Price is based on the number sold and early selection is recommended. Please return the attached form to receive additional information about specific images.

ACKNOWLEDGEMENTS

Many people have assisted in assembling the information contained in this book. In addition to contributing the book's introductory essay, Anita Ventura Mozley provided additional research to make the caption material more complete. Harry Smith's children, Robert and Audrey, were a great help in providing information about their father and the period of his life before their birth. They generously shared Harry Smith's own album of photographs, which provided specific dates and information about many of the images in the book. Arthur Andersen, Harry Smith's brother-in-law and the last surviving member of his generation, added some useful comments and identifications. Lawrence Dinnean of the University of California's Bancroft Library assisted in the identification of the photographs. Peter A. Andersen, the designer for the book, offered additional suggestions, as did David Featherstone, who helped in the preparation of the captions and text. My staff, Theresa Chavez and Joyce Dallal, helped to bring the flow of material together. My wife, Mus White, offered her critical eye and valuable suggestions about the photographs, while Richard Sullivan worked diligently to bring out the best possible quality in each negative. Finally, Shannon White, my daughter, put up with not seeing much of her father during the past several months.

Stephen White

128